everyday
STEM

SCIENCE

GEOLOGY

Science is all around you!

KINGFISHER
LONDON & NEW YORK

T0015819

KINGFISHER
LONDON & NEW YORK

Copyright © Macmillan Publishers International Ltd 2022, 2023
First published 2022
This edition published in the United States by Kingfisher
120 Broadway, New York, NY 10271
Kingfisher is an imprint of Macmillan Children's Books, London
All rights reserved.

Copyright © Macmillan Publishers International Ltd 2022, 2023

ISBN 978-0-7534-7744-1(HC)
978-0-7534-7745-8 (PB)

Distributed in the U.S. and Canada by Macmillan,
120 Broadway, New York, NY 10271

Library of Congress Cataloging-in-Publication data has been applied for.

Author: Emily Dodd
Illustrator: Robbie Cathro
Series editor: Lizzie Davey
Series design: Jim Green

Kingfisher Books are available for special promotions and premiums.
For details contact:
Special Markets Department, Macmillan
120 Broadway, New York, NY 10271.

For more information please visit:
www.kingfisherbooks.com

Printed in China
2 4 6 8 9 7 5 3 1
1TR/0923/UG/WKT/128MA

EU representative: 1st Floor, The Liffey Trust Centre
117-126 Sheriff Street Upper, Dublin 1 D01 YC43

CONTENTS

WHAT IS GEOLOGY?

Geology is all around you, from tiny components inside your phone to giant craters on the Moon. It's about finding clues in rocks and the landscape to make a story of how planet Earth works. How it moves, shakes, creates, and destroys. How mountains erode into sand and seafloors split open to make new land. Geology literally rocks!

GEOLOGY DEFINED

The word "geology" comes from the Greek words "ge" (meaning rocks or earth) and "logos" (meaning knowledge). It is the science and history of how Earth was formed, how its surface has changed, and what processes cause it to change today. Scientists who study geology are called geologists.

Concrete surfaces contain stones that were grated off rocks by ancient snowy glaciers. The stones were deposited in rivers and then collected by us thousands of years later, in a process called dredging.

JAMES HUTTON
(1726–1797)

James Hutton's discoveries were so important that he is known as the father of modern geology. Hutton realized that what he observed happening on Earth must have happened before, and that rocks were continually being recycled. He watched mountains erode into sediments and sediments being washed down rivers into seas. He realized that seabeds were being squashed into future rock as layers were added on top of them, and that these beds were later uplifted into mountains and volcanoes. Hutton's discoveries proved that Earth was much older than people had previously thought.

"THE PAST HISTORY OF OUR GLOBE MUST BE EXPLAINED BY WHAT CAN BE SEEN TO BE HAPPENING NOW."

 EROSION, SEDIMENTATION, AND UPLIFT!

The screen of this cell phone was made from granite mountains, which were weathered into tiny pieces of quartz sand. The sand traveled to the ocean to be collected, heated, and melted into glass by humans.

The plastic in this pen was made from tiny ancient sea creatures, which were buried and squashed deep underground. Millions of years later, we drilled them out as oil and then heated the oil to make plastic.

EARTH SCIENCE

Geology is part of a group of sciences known as Earth sciences. Earth science includes Earth's physical structure, its water systems, and the air around it. You've probably heard of two important Earth sciences: oceanography is the study of the world's oceans, and meteorology is the study of Earth's weather and atmosphere. Geologists use all kinds of equipment to help them with their work.

GEOLOGIST'S TOOLS

How many of these tools can you find on the page?

COMPASS CLINOMETER
Used to measure the angle and direction of rock layers.

MAP
A basic map that a geological map can be created on top of.

HAND LENS
Magnifies crystals and grains in a rock to help identify it.

MICROSCOPE
Magnifies and lights up thin sections of rock.

GEOLOGICAL HAMMER
Chips off small samples of rock to take away and identify later.

HYDROCHLORIC ACID
Used to test if a rock contains calcite. It will fizz on contact.

PAINTBRUSH
Used to carefully brush dirt off delicate fossils without damaging them.

HARD HAT
Protects your head from falling rocks, sand, and gravel.

NOTEBOOK AND PENCIL
Essential for recording information, drawing rocks, and making notes.

STRONG BOOTS
Support feet, keeping them dry in all weather.

GEOLOGICAL MAP
Locates rocks and other geological features.

CAMERA
Takes pictures of rocks and geological structures.

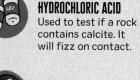

GEOLOGY JOBS

There are many exciting jobs that require a background knowledge of geology. Here are some of the awesome things geologists do:

VOLCANOLOGIST

Measures temperatures and observes gas at volcanoes to help monitor them and predict the next eruption.

PALEONTOLOGIST

Excavates and analyzes fossils to help identify and date the layers of rocks in an area.

ARCHAEOLOGIST

Uses magnets and electricity to see the differences in layers beneath Earth's surface in order to find archaeological remains.

SEISMOLOGIST

Uses earthquake and tsunami data to help predict where future tsunami waves will hit.

HYDROGEOLOGIST

Tests a water supply to make sure that chemicals from a nearby mine haven't escaped and polluted it.

GEOMORPHOLOGIST

Measures cliff-top erosion and models beach movement to predict when cliffs might collapse.

TYPES OF ROCK

There are three types of rock: sedimentary, igneous, and metamorphic. Sedimentary rocks are made from grains of rock that sank to the bottom of water and were buried by more layers. Igneous rocks are rocks that were previously melted into a liquid. Metamorphic rocks are sedimentary or igneous rocks that have been squeezed and heated (but not melted) into new rocks.

SEDIMENTARY

These rocks contain grains of sediment squashed together. They can contain pebbles, crushed shells, bones, pieces of coral, and fish poop.

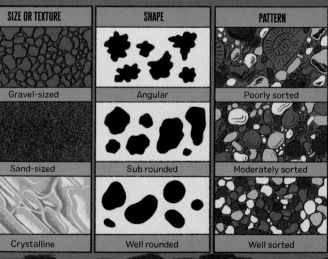

SANDSTONE

Microscope view

Sandstone contains sand-sized grains. They include sand, rock, and dead pieces of plants and animals, stuck together with smaller grains of mud.

SHALE
Shale is made from fine grains that were once mud.

LIMESTONE
Limestone is formed in calm, shallow tropical seas.

AMMONITE
Fossils, such as this one, help geologists date rocks.

MOHS HARDNESS SCALE

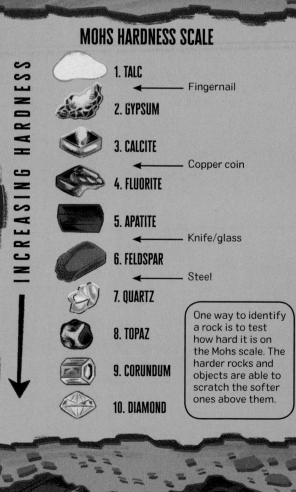

INCREASING HARDNESS

1. TALC — Fingernail
2. GYPSUM
3. CALCITE — Copper coin
4. FLUORITE
5. APATITE — Knife/glass
6. FELDSPAR — Steel
7. QUARTZ
8. TOPAZ
9. CORUNDUM
10. DIAMOND

One way to identify a rock is to test how hard it is on the Mohs scale. The harder rocks and objects are able to scratch the softer ones above them.

GRAIN CLASSIFICATION

Geologists look at the size, shape, and pattern of grains in sedimentary rock to identify the rock and determine what conditions were like in the water when the sediment was laid down.

SIZE OR TEXTURE	SHAPE	PATTERN
Gravel-sized	Angular	Poorly sorted
Sand-sized	Sub rounded	Moderately sorted
Crystalline	Well rounded	Well sorted

METAMORPHIC

When rocks are heated and squashed deep inside Earth, they deform and change, becoming harder versions of the original rock.

SLATE

Microscope view

Slate has hard layers that were once soft clay. Metamorphic rocks often have grains that all go the same way, because they've been pushed into line.

QUARTZITE
Pure quartz sandstone gets metamorphosed into quartzite.

GNEISS
This can form from igneous or sedimentary rock.

SCHIST
Schists are mud and shale that were squashed and heated.

HOW IS IT FORMED?
Metamorphic rock is formed deep inside Earth, when the crust moves around. It's also formed when melted rock pushes its way up through layers of sedimentary rock, squashing and folding them.

Hot, melted rock

Metamorphic rock is formed

Layers of sedimentary rock

ROCK CYCLE

Different types of rock are continually being created and remade in a never-ending process called the rock cycle. Mountains made of igneous rock are broken into tiny pieces by ice, water, and wind. These pieces travel through rivers and get dropped off in oceans. They form layers of sediment that are buried and become sedimentary rock. These get squashed and folded into new mountains, and the cycle begins again.

WEATHERING
Weather breaks rocks down in two ways. Ice, wind, and water physically break them up. Chemicals erode them—for example, acid in rain dissolves rock.

TRANSPORT
Transport is the movement of rock and sediments from one place to another. For example, a river rolls pebbles downstream.

SEDIMENTATION
Grains of sand and mud (sediments) that were floating in the water sink to the bottom and gather together.

SEDIMENTARY ROCK
As more sediment lands on top of previous layers, the oldest layers get squashed deep underground. They turn into sedimentary rock.

DEPOSITION
Water, wind, and ice all carry and drop off sediments. Putting down sediments after carrying them is called deposition.

SEAFLOOR SPREADING
The crust pulls apart and basalt lava fills the gap. This creates new seafloor at the bottom of the ocean, along a spreading ridge.

EROSION
Erosion is a process that moves pieces of rock and sand that have previously been broken down by weathering. It changes the shape of the landscape.

IGNEOUS ROCK
When liquid rock cools and hardens, it becomes igneous rock. This can happen to lava underwater or on the surface after a volcanic eruption. Igneous rock can also form when magma solidifies underground.

EXTRUSION
Magma comes to Earth's surface through cracks and volcanic vents. This is called extrusion. Lava, gas, and ash can all come out of a volcano during an eruption.

VOLCANO

CRYSTALLIZATION
When magma cools underground, crystals form, making new rock. The more slowly it cools, the bigger the crystals that form.

CONTINENTAL CRUST

OCEANIC CRUST

MAGMA
When liquid rock is beneath Earth's surface, we call it magma. Magma and gas rise up, creating volcanoes.

SUBDUCTION ZONE
The thinner layer of oceanic crust sinks below a thicker layer of continental crust. It makes the rock melt.

METAMORPHIC ROCK
Here, rock layers are heated and folded but not melted. This process changes igneous and sedimentary rocks into metamorphic rocks.

PLATE TECTONICS

Over time, tiny movements of rock caused by the rock cycle have changed the face of Earth. Huge chunks of land have slowly moved around like giant puzzle pieces, creating the continents we have today.

EARTH TODAY

250 MILLION YEARS AGO

EARTH'S STRUCTURE

Earth is formed of three layers: the crust, the mantle, and the core. The crust is the outer layer of solid rock that we stand on. Oceans float on top of it in some places. The mantle below is solid rock, but it moves—it flows very slowly. The outer core is liquid metal, and the inner core is solid metal.

INNER CORE
Solid metal

OUTER CORE
Liquid metal

MANTLE
Rock

CRUST
Rock

CONTINENTAL CRUST
Up to 55 mi. (90 km) thick and made of granite.

OCEANIC CRUST
Just a few miles thick and made of basalt.

MELT ZONE
This layer contains partly melted mantle rock.

LOWER MANTLE
Solid rock that flows very slowly.

OUTER CORE

INNER CORE

IF EARTH WAS THE SIZE OF AN APPLE, ITS CRUST WOULD BE THE THICKNESS OF AN APPLE'S SKIN

FLORENCE BASCOM (1862–1945)

Florence Bascom was a pioneer in geological science.

She was a professor of geology at Bryn Mawr College in Pennsylvania from 1895 to 1928 . . .

. . . and a researcher with the U.S. Geological Survey from 1896 to 1936.

Bascom was an authority on the crystalline rocks of the Piedmont area of the Appalachian Mountains.

Some of her surveys are still used by geologists today.

Bascom helped train most of the U.S. female geologists of her time.

She advanced the role of women in science, especially in scientific field work, at a time when it was considered man's work.

"When any woman manifests an interest in the science [of geology] I am always glad to tell her of its possibilities and she makes her own choice. Not only must a girl have the mental aptitude for scientific research, but also physical strength and great physical courage."

GEOLOGY IN YOUR PHONE

Your cell phone is a tiny treasure chest full of geology. It includes valuable metals that are mined and extracted from rocks called ore. There are silver, or tin, and copper connectors gluing things together. Your phone screen is made from melted sand, and the plastic parts in your phone were made from oil.

SOLDER

Made from: Tin or silver

The metal connections in the phone are stuck together with hot liquid metal called solder. It hardens as it cools and can conduct electricity. Solder is made from tin or silver. Both metals are mined as ores.

COPPER CONNECTORS

Made from: Chalcopyrite

Copper conducts electricity and bends easily, so it's used to make wires for electronics. Chalcopyrite is one common copper ore. It's also called peacock ore because of its beautiful colors.

SILICON CHIPS

Made from: Quartzite

Silicon chips are made of melted sand. But unlike the glass screen, this sand needs to be pure quartz, not just beach sand. Quartzite is sandstone that's been metamorphosed.

PHONE CASING

Made from: Bauxite

The aluminum for the phone casing is extracted from a rock called bauxite using lots of energy. Bauxite is a sedimentary rock that can be crumbly or solid. It formed from sediments in a tropical place.

DEEP SEA MINING

Deep under the sea, metals deposit around hydrothermal vents. These vents form when water gets heated by volcanic rocks. In the future we may mine them for cell phone parts!

ORES

An ore is a rock from which metal can be extracted. For example, iron comes from iron ore.

PHONE SCREEN

Made from: Sand

The strengthened glass to make your phone screen is made from a weathered igneous rock—granite—which has broken down into quartz sand. These tiny grains of quartz are heated into glass. Aluminum is added for strength.

BATTERY

Made from: Lithium

The lithium metal for a rechargeable battery comes from two places. Lithium brine was concentrated into rocks called evaporites in salty ancient seas. Lithium is also formed deep inside Earth, in igneous rocks called pegmatites.

OIL FORMATION

1. Plankton dies
Tiny marine animals called plankton die, then sink to the bottom of an ocean or swamp. Layers of sediment fall on top of them, and they get buried deeper and deeper underground.

2. Oil forms
Over millions of years, the heat and pressure underground squash the layer of plankton, and they turn into oil and natural gas, which move upward through porous rock (rock with holes in it).

← Oil

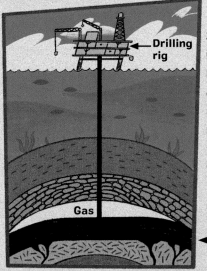

Drilling rig →

3. Drilling out oil
Over time the rocks bend. The rising oil and gas stop when they reach a solid layer of rock. We drill through this rock and pump water into the oil. Oil floats on water, so it rises to the surface.

Gas

← Oil

FROM PLANKTON TO PLASTIC

Plastic is a revolutionary invention. It can hold liquids and chemicals without reacting, and it doesn't shatter like glass or ceramics. Single-use plastic pollution is a big problem, but there are many things to thank plastic for—such as bike helmets, space suits, and blood transfusion bags — they're all fantastic plastic. Here's how a plastic bottle is made, from prehistoric plankton to finished product.

TRANSPORTATION

The oil that has been pumped out is known as crude oil. It gets pumped into a big ship called an oil tanker, which transports it from the drilling rig to an oil refinery on land. The crude oil may travel through a pipeline on land too.

MAKING A PLASTIC PRODUCT

Liquid plastic

Air

Cut off

Mold

1 2 3 4

The polyethylene pellets are shipped to another factory. They get melted and sucked into an injection mold. Air is pumped in to push the plastic into the shape of the mold. Once the plastic is cool, the mold is removed—a bottle has been made.

REFINING CRUDE OIL

Refinery gases

70°F (20°C)
160°F (70°C)

Gasoline

250°F (120°C)

Naphtha

400°F (200°C)

Kerosene

570°F (300°C)

Diesel

700°F (375°C)

Fuel oil

Bitumen

Crude oil enters

The oil is heated

Crude oil consists of lots of liquids mixed together. To separate them, we heat the oil so it all evaporates into a gas. The different liquids then condense, or turn from gas to liquid, at different temperatures. As the oil cools, liquids are piped off the column at different heights.

POLYMERIZATION

Cracking makes something called fluff, which looks like laundry detergent. It is heated and mixed with chemicals to make polyethylene plastic, which is cut into little pellets.

CRACKING

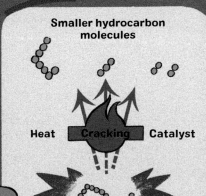

Smaller hydrocarbon molecules

Heat Cracking Catalyst

Large hydrocarbon molecule

Naphtha contains long chains of hydrogen and carbon atoms. These get split (or cracked) into smaller pieces. A catalyst is added to speed up the reaction.

ALUMINUM CAN

When you open a soda can and hear the bubbles fizz, do you ever stop to think about geology? The aluminum that makes your can is the most common metal on Earth, but it's not easy to get to. Aluminum isn't found naturally as pure lumps of metal. Instead it's mixed into soil and rock in an ore. Bauxite is a sedimentary rock, and it's the most common ore we extract aluminum from. Going from rock to can uses huge amounts of energy.

EXTRACTION

First geologists drill to test the soil and see if there's bauxite. If they find enough, mining begins. Bulldozers and explosives loosen the rock, then excavators collect it and load it into trucks.

Drilling ←

PROCESSING PLANT

The extracted bauxite is transported to a processing plant, where it is refined and then smelted to make pure aluminum. On arrival, the bauxite is ground up and chemicals are added to it.

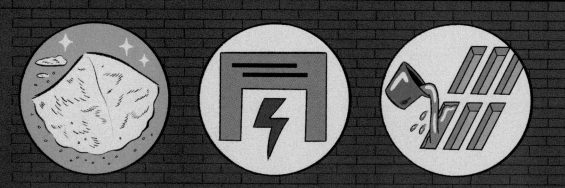

REFINING

The ground-up bauxite is steamed and filtered to create a fine white powder called alumina.

SMELTING

Alumina is heated to 1,800°F (1,000°C) and electricity is used to separate pure aluminum from alumina.

CASTING

Liquid aluminum is poured into molds. It cools, forming solid aluminum bars.

STORES

The cans are sent to stores and put in refrigerators. A can may have traveled between several different countries on its journey from the ground.

DRINKS COMPANY

The open cans are transported to a drinks company. They are filled with carbonated liquid by a machine, and the tops are attached and sealed on.

RECYCLING

We can make 20 recycled cans with the same energy it takes to make one can from scratch! Aluminum doesn't degrade when it gets remelted, so it can be recycled over and over again.

FACTORY

The aluminum bars are transported to another factory, where they are rolled out, cut up, and made into cans.

ROLLED INTO SHEETS

The aluminum bars are heated to soften the metal. Once soft, the bars are rolled out, making big, thin sheets of aluminum.

MADE INTO CAN

Machines shape the aluminum into a can without a top. The can is cleaned several times, including by washing it with acid!

CONCRETE

Concrete is hard, strong, and very useful. More than two-thirds of Earth's population lives in concrete buildings. The first concrete structures, made by the Romans, are still standing. You may have ridden your bike on a concrete road or traveled through a concrete tunnel, but did you wonder how it was made and where the ingredients came from? The geological processes that made these ingredients happened over millions of years.

SAND

Sand is tiny bits of eroded rock. Weather wears down mountains, breaking pieces off that travel along in rivers. The pieces get smaller as they bash against each other in the water, until they are tiny grains of sand.

GRAVEL

Gravel is small pieces of rock. It can be formed when larger rocks are broken up in rivers or by glaciers. Gravel can also be created by using machines to crush bigger rocks into pieces called aggregates.

CEMENT

Cement is a powder made from crushed limestone and clay. The limestone gets heated up with the clay and then ground down. Clay was once mud deposited in riverbeds. Limestone is a sedimentary rock.

WHERE DO THE INGREDIENTS COME FROM?

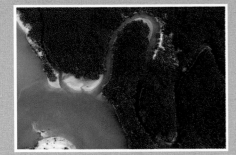

Sand Most building sand is dug up from riverbeds.

Gravel Moving glaciers grate pieces of gravel off bigger rocks.

Limestone Cement is made from limestone, which we quarry.

WATER

Water turns the dry ingredients into concrete. It changes the cement into a binder in a chemical reaction—the water and cement become the glue that holds everything else together.

CONCRETE

Once poured, the liquid concrete is vibrated to get rid of any air bubbles. Then it sets, becoming solid and very strong. It can be made at different strengths depending on exactly what goes into the mixture.

WE MAKE TWICE AS MUCH CONCRETE AS PLASTIC, STEEL, AND ALUMINUM COMBINED.

PLATE TECTONICS

Earth's rocky outer layer, the crust, is split into giant pieces called tectonic plates. The plates move in different directions, at about the same speed your fingernails grow. Most volcanic activity and earthquakes occur at the boundaries between the plates.

EXPLOSIVE VOLCANO

When plates move toward each other, the thinner oceanic plate slides under the thick continental plate. The thinner plate melts, allowing magma to rise up and explode through the surface.

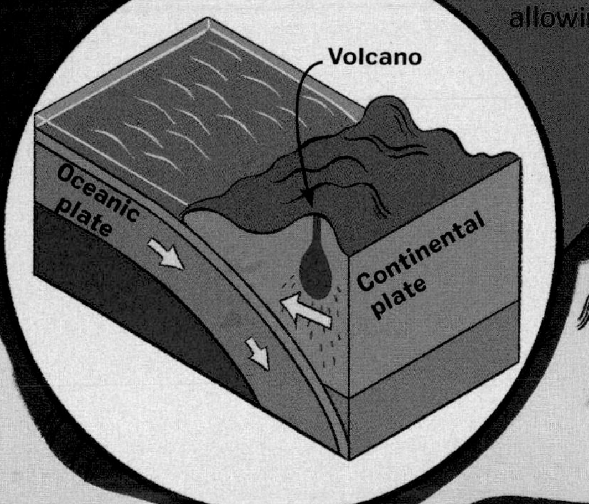

Volcano

Oceanic plate

Continental plate

Island chain

Active volcano

Magma chamber

HOTSPOT VOLCANO

Not all volcanoes are at plate boundaries. Hot magma can rise and punch through a moving plate, making a volcanic island and later an island chain.

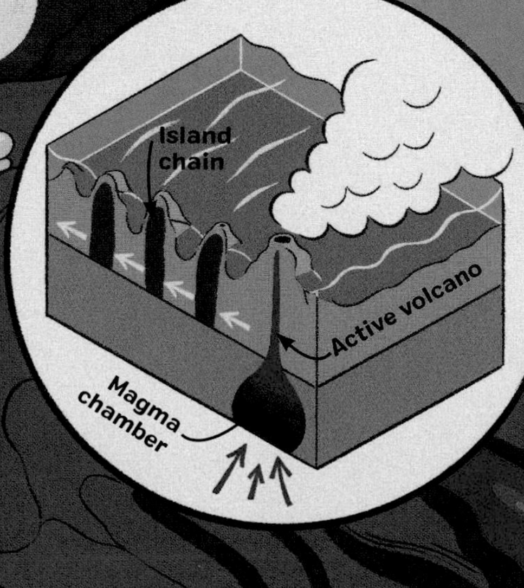

New crust forms

Magma

EFFUSIVE VOLCANO

Effusive (or runny) volcanoes happen when plates move away from each other. Runny lava spills out in the gap between the plates, making new crust.

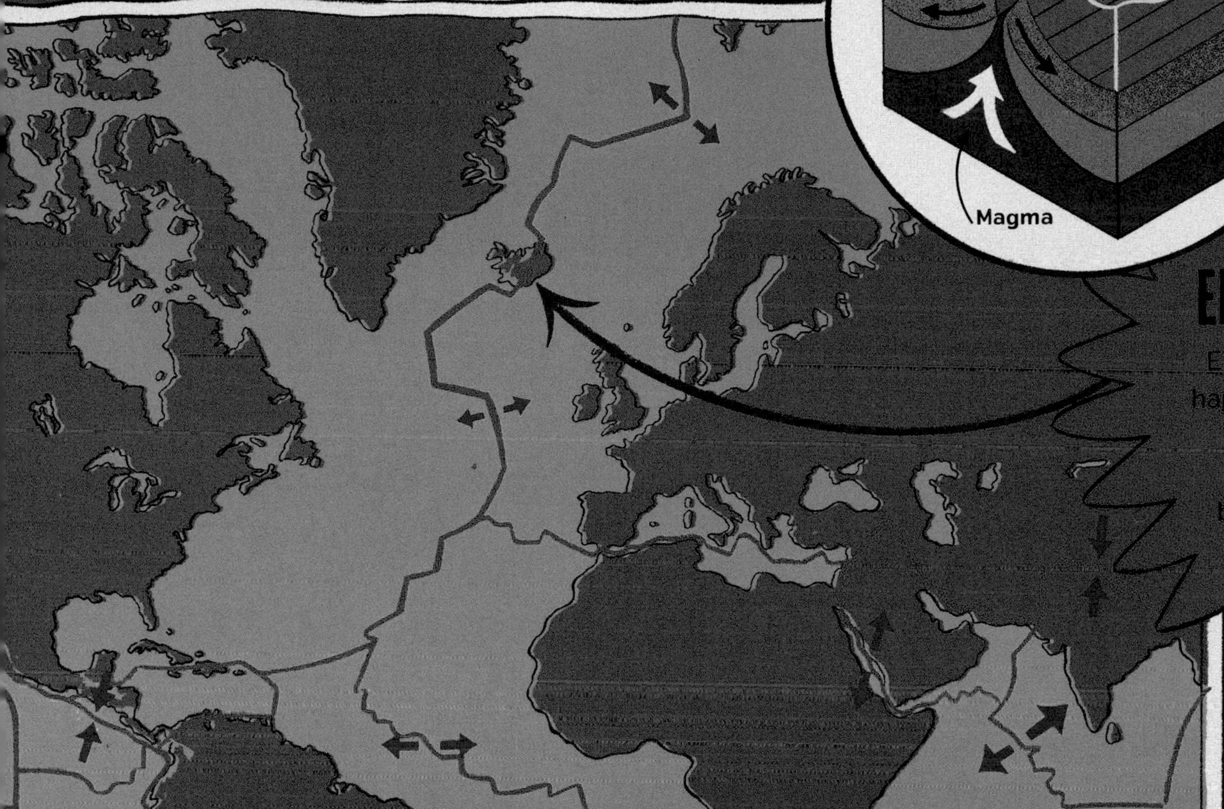

N

MAP KEY

PLATE BOUNDARIES
The area where tectonic plates meet each other.

PLATE MOVEMENT
As plates move, they trigger earthquakes and volcanic activity.

EARTHQUAKES

The huge puzzle pieces of rock that make up the surface of Earth are constantly moving in different directions. Earthquakes happen when the plates crumple and spring back, or when friction sticks moving plates together until they suddenly jolt forward.

EPICENTER NEAR EARTH'S SURFACE
The place on the surface directly above the focus.

WAVES
Earthquake waves travel inside Earth and along the surface.

FAULT
The line the movement happens along.

FOCUS
The place where the earthquake begins.

WOAH!

PREDICTING EARTHQUAKES

Earthquakes are really hard to predict! We know where they're likely to happen—along plate boundaries. But knowing when is more difficult. One way to predict when is to record how often earthquakes take place and assume the pattern will continue.

FAULT MOTION

There are three ways rock can move along a fault. Faulting can be large scale, when an entire plate moves, or it can involve smaller pieces of moving rock.

STRIKE SLIP Rock moves horizontally along one side of a vertical fault.

NORMAL Where the rock above the fault drops downward past the block below.

REVERSE (OR THRUST) This is like normal, but with movement in the opposite direction—the rock above the fault lifts.

The ground shakes, moving the frame from left to right.

Weight

Pen

The drum rotates a paper roll, which records movement over time.

SEISMOMETERS

This simple seismometer measures earthquake size and duration. During an earthquake, the ground moves from side to side. The frame moves, while the pen stays almost stationary. As the drum turns, the pen draws how big the earthquake vibrations are.

SEEING INSIDE EARTH

Every time there's an earthquake, we measure the vibrations using seismometers all over Earth. We measure two types of waves made by earthquakes—P waves and S waves. Combining these measurements helps us figure out what is inside Earth.

P WAVE

These are vibrations that squash and unsquash the material they are traveling through. They change direction when they travel between solids and liquids. Measuring them allows us to determine what Earth's layers are made of.

S WAVE

S waves are side-to-side wiggles also known as shear waves. They move more slowly than P waves and do not travel through liquid. The S wave shadow zone (the area the waves don't reach) shows us that Earth has a liquid outer core.

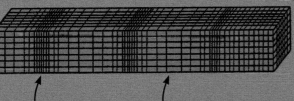

Squashed area   Unsquashed area

Side to side wiggle

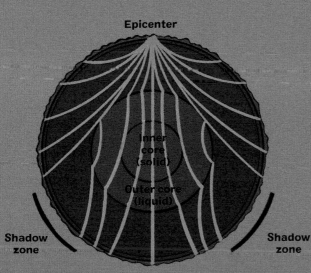

Epicenter

Inner core (solid)

Outer core (liquid)

Shadow zone

Shadow zone

Epicenter

Inner core (solid)

Outer core (liquid)

Shadow zone

GEOLOGICAL MAPS

Geological maps show different types of rocks in different colors, along with features such as fault lines, landslides, and fossils. The angle and direction of rocks are included so geologists can use the map data to figure out how rocks continue underground. Geological maps are used to plan mines, buildings, and transportation lines. They help predict earthquakes, volcanoes, and landslides. Making a map is something all geologists learn to do.

TOPOGRAPHY

Geological maps show height changes in the landscape—this is called topography. One way geologists measure heights is by using a measuring stick. They start from a known location and height, then read heights from the stick. Any changes in height are added to the map.

OUTCROPS

Areas where rocks are visible at the surface are called outcrops. To map them, geologists need to identify which types of rocks they are. To help, they use tools including hand lenses, Mohs hardness scale, and hydrochloric acid. They might also draw a sketch of the rocks or hammer off a sample to identify later.

WILLIAM SMITH (1769–1839)

William Smith was a canal surveyor who single-handedly mapped the geology of the UK, creating the first useful geological map in the world! Smith studied rocks because he needed to plan where to dig canals. He loved fossils and used them to help date rock layers. His map was valuable because it also showed where to mine for coal, oil, iron, tin, and even diamonds.

Life wasn't easy for Smith, however. His map was stolen and copied, he had to sell all of his possessions to fund his work, and he was put in prison for owing money. Eventually he was freed and recognized as the true creator of the map. It was published in 1815.

"IF TWO LAYERS OF ROCK HAVE THE SAME FOSSILS, THEY MUST BE THE SAME AGE!"

COMPASS CLINOMETER

This tool measures angles as well as direction. These "dip and strike" measurements are added to the map. Dip direction is the downward angle in which a rock tilts. Strike is at right angles to dip. Together these measurements describe how a rock slopes.

MONITORING A VOLCANO

Geologists who study volcanoes are called volcanologists. Active volcanoes are dangerous, so volcanologists use tools and technology to help them monitor volcanoes from a safe distance. Earthquake vibrations, temperature changes, gas emissions, and land movements are all clues that suggest a volcano might erupt. Volcanologists study all these clues, as well as eruption data from volcanoes all over Earth. Their findings are used to help predict eruptions, make evacuation plans, and save lives.

HERE IS SOME AMAZING VOLCANO-MONITORING EQUIPMENT!

THERMAL IMAGING CAMERA

This camera takes pictures of the heat waves emitted by volcanoes. Volcanologists can observe temperature changes, showing them which lava flows are hotter and therefore newer. When magma starts to rise through the main vent, the overall temperature of the volcano increases, making an eruption more likely.

GPS AND TILTMETERS

The sides of a volcano often bulge or spread apart when It Is about to erupt. Tiltmeters have a bubble in them, like a spirit level, which moves with the slightest change in the tilt of the slope. GPS stations are placed around the volcano and monitored to see if they move away from each other as the ground expands.

KATIA KRAFFT
(1942–1991)

Katia Krafft and her husband, Maurice, were brave enough to study, film, and photograph volcanic eruptions up close before we had the technology to take measurements from a distance. They studied lava flows, ash, acid rain, and new types of volcanoes. They wore lava bomb helmets and used riot shields to protect themselves from volcanic debris. The couple started a volcano center, wrote many books on volcanoes, and made a TV documentary. Sadly, they were killed in the course of their research by a lava flow that changed direction unexpectedly.

GAS EMISSIONS

A robot called a "spider" can be dropped into a volcano. It monitors the gases escaping from a volcano, such as hydrogen sulfide, which would indicate an impending eruption. Gas can also be measured safely from a distance using a device called a spectrometer. It looks like a telescope and measures the UV light absorbed by different gases.

RADAR

Radio waves can be used to make detailed 3D maps of a volcano's surface. These maps are used to predict lava flow patterns. Radar can also be used to detect any volcanic height changes.

DRONES

Remote-controlled drones can fly in close and film a volcano. A drone can also carry sulfur dioxide sensors, particle sensors, and air-sampling bottles.

STUDYING FOSSILS

Fossils are clues that tell us about life in the past. They tell us which life forms existed, how they lived, what they ate for dinner, and even what the weather was like around them! Geologists who specialize in studying fossils are called paleontologists. Paleontologists learn which life forms lived at different times so they can use fossils to help them date rocks.

FOSSILIZATION

Fossils are the preserved remains of life forms, or the evidence left behind by life. Hard parts like bones and shells can become fossilized. But so can animal tracks and signs—for example, burrows, nests, poop, and footprints. Here's how one dinosaur became fossilized.

The dinosaur died in or near water. Its skeleton was quickly buried in sand.

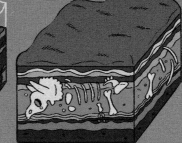

Sediment layers built up, squashing the lower layers into rock. Mineral in water dissolved the bones and hardened to stone, creating a fossil.

Millions of years later, the rock around the bones was uplifted, revealing the fossil.

MARY ANNING (1799–1847)

Mary grew up by the sea in Lyme Regis, England. Her father collected and sold fossils. He died when she was just 11, but Mary continued the family business with her older brother. Together they discovered something wonderful—a huge marine reptile called an ichthyosaur. The ichthyosaur was so big that they had to pay people to dig it out. They sold it to their landlord for £23, which would be around £1,800 today. Mary loved to draw fossils, and there's a tongue twister about her—can you say, "She sells seashells by the seashore"?

DATING ROCKS

Fossils can be used to help date layers of sedimentary rock because different plants and animals were alive during different geological time periods. For example, *triceratops* lived in the Cretaceous period. Here are some examples of different types of fossils:

Body
The hard parts of living things preserved as stone— for example, shells, bones, and teeth.

Mold and cast
A mold is a negative impression made by a living thing. A cast is a filled-in mold.

True form
A completely preserved living thing, including the soft parts. This is rare, but can happen in tar, peat, ice, and amber.

Trace
The tracks or signs left behind by living things— for example, nests, burrows, and footprints.

HOLOCENE

PLEISTOCENE

PLIOCENE

MIOCENE

OLIGOCENE

EOCENE

PALEOCENE

CRETACEOUS

JURASSIC

TRIASSIC

PERMIAN

PENNSYLVANIAN

MISSISSIPPIAN

DEVONIAN

SILURIAN

ORDOVICIAN

CAMBRIAN

PROTEROZOIC (2.5 BILLION– 542 MILLION YEARS AGO)

ARCHEAN (4.6–2.5 BILLION YEARS AGO)

CENOZOIC (66 MILLION YEARS AGO–TODAY)

MESOZOIC (252–66 MILLION YEARS AGO)

PALEOZOIC (542–252 MILLION YEARS AGO)

LIFE IN THE PAST

Paleontologists piece together evidence from different fossil discoveries. They also compare fossil remains to plants and animals that are alive today to help them understand about life in the past. Here are some examples of bones and traces of life from millions of years ago—and how they can tell us what life was actually like.

ANIMAL BEHAVIOR

Parts of animals' bodies can tell us about how they lived. For example, a *T. rex* tooth found embedded in another dinosaur's tail tells us that *T. rex* was a hunter.

VELOCIRAPTOR CLAW
Sharp claws and teeth are used by carnivores—this was a meat eater.

WOOLLY MAMMOTH TOOTH
This huge flat tooth was used to grind plants—this was a herbivore.

APATOSAURUS LEG BONE
This thigh bone is almost 6.5 feet (2 m) long, so we know this dinosaur was tall.

T. REX SKULL
Cavities in a skull show us how big the brain, nose, and eyes were.

PLANT FOSSIL
Plant remains show us what herbivores ate and how plants evolved.

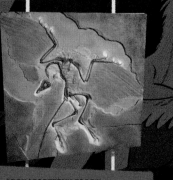

ARCHAEOPTERYX FOSSIL
This dinosaur had feathers, showing us that dinosaurs are related to birds.

INSECTS
Insects appear in the fossil record at the same time plants started flowering.

BRACHIOPOD SHELL
These creatures lived in the sea, so we use them to map prehistoric oceans.

GEORGES CUVIER
(1769–1832)

Georges Cuvier was a French zoologist and animal anatomy expert. He taught at the Museum of Natural History in Paris. Cuvier could draw what an animal looked like, often from just a few bones. He began to use his skills to study fossils, drawing what a prehistoric reptile or mammal might have looked like based on its fossils. This is how the science of paleontology began.

STEGOSAURUS PLATES
Why did *Stegosaurus* have plates? We don't know, and scientists are still guessing.

TRACES OF LIFE
Not all fossils are the remains of living things. Some show indirect evidence of life, such as footprints where a dinosaur once walked.

RIPPLES
Patterns of ripples show us how and where ancient water flowed.

COPROLITE
Fossilized pieces of poop, called coprolites, can show us what animals ate.

TREE RINGS
We count tree rings to age a tree. They also show us how climates have changed.

NESTS
These show us that dinosaurs laid eggs. Some contain fossilized babies.

BURROWS
Worms are soft, so we don't find their bodies, but we have found their burrows.

ENVIRONMENTAL IMPACT

Mining for metals and coal changes the landscape and creates problems that can last long after a mine has closed. Rain water mixes with piles of mining waste, creating pools of weak sulfuric acid. Acidic soil and lakes are bad news for plants, animals, and humans living nearby, especially if the acid and metals get into the water system. Here's how geologists solve some of the problems mining creates.

NATURAL SOLUTION

Gravity and plants can purify water! By using the natural shape of the landscape and digging extra channels, it's possible to direct polluted water through a series of reed beds. These plants filter out metals and reduce acid. This technique can remove only small amounts of pollution.

An open-cast metal mine

CREATING GREEN SPACES

Hard work by officials and conservation charities can reverse the damage caused by mining. Former open-cast mines are converted into beautiful nature reserves with reed beds, woods, lakes, and islands—spaces for humans and other animals to enjoy.

ZELMA MAINE JACKSON

Zelma Maine Jackson is an American exploration geologist. She worked to clean up ground water in Washington State by removing nuclear waste. Jackson advocates for people in communities affected by hazardous waste. In her early career, she spent time on drill rigs searching for uranium by analyzing drill cores in the Rocky Mountains. She also saves sea turtles in her spare time!

CHEMICAL SOLUTION

Ground up limestone is used to treat acid lakes at many mines. Acid is neutralized when we add an alkali to it, and limestone is alkaline. It makes dissolved metals precipitate out of the water, turning them into a toxic sludge that can be removed. But not all mines have limestone outcrops nearby.

BIOLOGICAL SOLUTION

Bacteria are tiny, one-celled living things. Some of them eat toxins, including acid. If geologists add the correct bacteria to an acidic lake, the bacteria eat toxins from the water, reducing its acidity. This solution is called bioremediation.

GEOENGINEERING

We are in a climate crisis! Humans have been adding large quantities of carbon dioxide into the air for 300 years. This "greenhouse gas" traps the Sun's heat in our atmosphere, warming our planet. Climate change threatens food, water, wildlife, and ecosystems. Geoengineering is the adaptation of the environment's processes to stop climate change. There are two main ways to do this: by reflecting sunlight away from Earth and by removing carbon dioxide from the air and oceans.

REFLECT SUNLIGHT

Reflecting sunlight back into space could reduce rising temperatures. To do this, we could put giant mirrors in orbit around Earth, paint our roofs white, or genetically modify crops to make them paler and more reflective. Another idea is cloud seeding—making white reflective clouds by spraying seawater high into the atmosphere.

Cloud seeding

FEED ALGAE

Algae take in carbon dioxide, which gets trapped as ocean sediments when they die. Adding iron or nitrogen to the oceans feeds algae, allowing them to multiply and trap more carbon. Algal blooms can harm marine ecosystems, so the aim is to engineer new, safer types of algae.

ANTHROPOCENE

Humans have changed three-fourths of Earth's non-ice surface area. We have chopped down trees, created farms, and built huge cities. Over time, this human activity has made millions of plant and animal species extinct. The human-caused changes are so great that we have now begun a new geological time period—the Anthropocene.

COPY A VOLCANO

Spraying sulfate particles into the air mimics a volcanic eruption. The particles reflect sunlight and could drop global temperatures by 5.4°F (3°C). This could only be a temporary solution, as airplanes would need to constantly spray particles into the air to make it work.

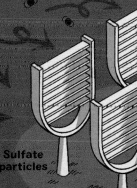

Sulfate particles

TREES TO THE RESCUE

Trees take in carbon dioxide from the air and release oxygen. When they die, their carbon is stored in the soil. Replanting the huge areas of forests that humans have chopped down—reforesting—would help reverse the climate crisis.

INCREASE WEATHERING

Rocks are gradually broken down by the weather in a process that uses carbon dioxide from the air. If we increase the surface area for weathering, more carbon dioxide can be removed. We can do this by spraying ground-up volcanic rock over the ground.

Pumping station adds carbon dioxide to the ground

GEOLOGY IN SPACE

Geological processes take place on other planets too! We can investigate geology in space by comparing the landforms there with those we see on Earth. Satellites and probes take pictures of other planets using light, radio waves, and heat waves. We study the photos and use them to identify lava flows, glaciers, rivers, valleys, and earthquake faults. We know what they look like because of how they look on Earth.

Tectonism The movement of tectonic plates, which creates folds, fractures, and faults.

Gradation The erosion, transportation, and deposition of materials due to water, ice, gravity, and wind.

Volcanism The movement of liquid rock onto or near Earth's surface, making new rock and surface features, such as these hot springs.

Impact craters Space rocks such as meteorites hit Earth's surface, leaving craters behind.

EARTH FIRST

These four geological processes have formed and reformed the surface of planet Earth. They have also shaped the surfaces of other planets and moons.

Volcanic plains
The dark areas of the Moon are stretches of lava formed by ancient volcanic eruptions.

Meteor craters
The Moon's surface is pitted with impact craters from meteorites and comets.

WATER ON EARTH
Rivers once flowed down this mountain in Iran, carving out channels that spread out into a fan shape, called an alluvial fan, at the bottom. The river channels are now dry, leaving patterns similar to those made by rivers on Mars.

Alluvial fan

EARTH'S MOON
Rocks and soil brought back from the Moon are similar to materials from Earth. It is covered in craters. Because it is so close to Earth, we can assume Earth was cratered too, before plate tectonics recycled our landscape.

River valley These patterns were made by water, showing us that there was once liquid water on Mars.

Olympus Mons This is an enormous volcano—it is more than 370 mi. (600 km) wide and 15 mi. (25 km) high.

MARS
Mars has been shaped by the four major geological processes: volcanism, gradation, tectonism, and impact craters. The main geological process on Mars today is gradation by landslides and wind.

Curiosity rover This robot vehicle travels across Mars taking photos, collecting samples, and studying rocks.

GEOPHYSICS

Using physics to study Earth's processes is called geophysics. Geophysicists can map rocks by detecting changes in the pattern of Earth's magnetic field. They can map the shape of the seabed using sound waves. They can even use satellites in space to collect electromagnetic waves given off by particular rocks. Here's some of the amazing technology geophysicists use.

SATELLITE

Satellites take photographs and videos and can be used to map geological structures. They can also bounce radio and light waves off the land to detect any structures hidden under plants.

GROUND PENETRATING RADAR

Ground penetrating radar sends radio waves through the ground and detects any echoes that bounce off hidden structures. The echoes help us determine what shape, size, and material any structures are.

RESISTIVITY

Electric currents are sent through the ground using a grid of electrodes and wires. Electricity flows at different rates when it moves through different materials, so we can detect where materials change below the surface.

AIRBORNE MAGNETOMETER

Magnetometers are towed along by helicopters to measure changes in Earth's magnetic field. Rocks have different amounts of magnetic minerals in them, so magnetometers can detect rock changes and structures, such as faults.

INFRARED IMAGERY

Every object glows with infrared light, which we can't see with our eyes. An infrared camera on a helicopter or satellite can see surface rock changes because different rocks emit and absorb different amounts of infrared light.

MAPPING IN 3D

Instead of one lone geologist making a paper map, a team of scientists can now add information to an online GPS-located map, which makes 3D models of the rocks beneath Earth's surface.

SIDE SCAN

A towed submersible sends high frequency sound pulses into the water that bounce back off any structures. The data collected is used to map the geology of the seabed and to find objects that are hidden underwater.

FOSSIL MAKING

Here's an experiment to show you how some fossils are formed. The salt dough represents mud, which then turns to rock over millions of years.

YOU WILL NEED
- 2 cups (250 g) all-purpose flour
- 1 cup (250 g) table salt
- ½ cup (125 ml) warm water
- A paper cup
- Seashells
- Plastic toys with feet
- Non-drying modeling clay

MAKE SALT DOUGH

1 Mix the flour and salt together.

2 Slowly add the water. Keep stirring it together until it forms a dough.

3 Place your dough on a lightly floured surface and spend eight minutes kneading it. This means pushing and stretching the dough until it becomes smooth and elastic.

TRACE FOSSIL

CAST FOSSIL

1. Squish non-drying modeling clay into the bottom of the paper cup and flatten it. Imagine it is mud or sand.

2. Use shells to make impressions in the clay.

3. Now add a layer of salt dough and press it down over the top. Imagine this is a layer of sediment being deposited on top of the layer of mud or sand.

4. Leave your cup to dry in a warm place for a couple of days.

5. Cut open the cup and remove the modeling clay. You will have a cast that was created when the salt dough filled the shell impression.

WOOSH

IMPACT CRATERS

Impact craters are created when meteorites hit planets and moons. This experiment will show you how crater shapes vary depending on how fast the meteorite hits.

YOU WILL NEED

- A tray
- Sand
- Flour
- A sieve
- Pebbles, marbles, or small heavy balls
- Safety goggles
- An elastic band or hair band

DIRECTIONS

1. Spread 1 in. (3 cm) of sand evenly across your tray. This represents rock.

2. Sift a thin layer of flour over the top, just enough to cover the sand below. This represents soil.

3. With an adult supervising, choose a marble or pebble to be your meteorite, and drop it from a set height, such as a table or desk, above your tray.

4. Look at the pattern your meteorite makes when it impacts.

5. Stay at the same height, but move above an undisturbed part of the tray. Stretch the elastic band between your finger and thumb and use it to launch your meteorite. It will move faster than the first meteorite.

6. Compare the two impact craters. The way the sand and flour move shows how topsoil and rock are displaced by a meteor impact.

TSUNAMIS IN THE TUB

Tsunamis are fast, powerful waves. They increase in height as they travel from deep ocean to land, causing flooding and devastation. Three-fourths of tsunamis are caused by earthquakes—this experiment shows you how. Reuse your bathwater for a tsunami experience!

YOU WILL NEED

- A large tray or plastic container
- An old towel
- A bathtub
- Water

DIRECTIONS

1. Place a tray underwater, flat on the bottom at one end of the bathtub.

2. Lay a towel down to the edge of the water at the other end of the tub. This is how you will measure wave height.

3. Put your hands into the water slowly, so that you don't make a wave. Then hold both sides of the tray. Your hands should be on the sides that are parallel to the long sides of the bathtub.

4. Experiment to see how high the waves go up the towel when you lift the tray:

- Halfway to the water's surface, slowly

- Halfway to the water's surface, quickly

- Halfway to the water's surface, even quicker

- All the way to the top, very quickly

The water will mark the towel, so you can compare how high each set of waves reaches.

Meteorite tsunami: Next time you're near a still lake, try throwing a pebble into the water. Watch how the ripples travel and get bigger as they come ashore. This is how some tsunamis are produced by meteorites!

STALACTITES & STALAGMITES

Stalactites and stalagmites are made when the minerals dissolved in water solidify, becoming rock again. Solids that form from solutions in this way are called precipitates. Here's an experiment to show this process.

DIRECTIONS

1. Fill both jars with hot water and place them on a tray with the saucer between them.

2. Stir baking soda into the water, a spoonful at a time. Dissolve as much baking soda as you can.

3. Twist several strands of yarn together. Place the ends of the yarn into the jars and weigh them down with pebbles. The yarn should dip down between the two jars, above the saucer.

4. Put the tray somewhere it will stay still. Your stalactites and stalagmites will appear over a few weeks, so be patient.

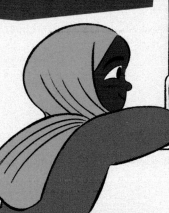

The water with baking soda dissolved in it will soak through the yarn and drip down onto the saucer. Then the baking soda precipitates back out of the water, making tiny stalactites and stalagmites. After a while, they might even join in the middle.

GLOSSARY AND CREDITS

Aggregate
Man-made crushed rock.

Atom
The smallest component of matter. Atoms can be combined to form molecules.

Bioremediation
When bacteria (or another living organism) is added to soil, water, or air to remove toxins and pollutants.

Catalyst
A substance that speeds up a chemical reaction.

Crude oil
Also called petroleum. A naturally occurring liquid found deep underground. It is used to make fuels and oils.

Crystal
The shape in which many minerals form. A crystal has fixed properties, and the sides are usually flat and regular.

Dredging
The removal of earth, sand, or gravel from the bottom of a riverbed or ocean floor.

Fault line
A line of movement where pieces of rock move past each other.

Infrared
A type of light energy that cannot be seen by the human eye.

Magma
Hot, liquid rock beneath Earth's surface. On the surface the same substance is called lava.

Magnetic field
The area surrounding a magnet, where the magnetic force acts. Earth has a magnetic field.

Metamorphic
A type of rock that has undergone a change—but not been melted—due to heat and pressure.

Meteorite
A lump of rock from space that hits Earth's surface.

Molecule
The smallest possible unit of a chemical.

Ore
Rock that can be heated or treated in other ways to yield metal or other valuable minerals.

Pyroclastic flow
A deadly volcanic flow full of ash, gas, and pieces of rock.

Sediment
Tiny pieces of rock and the remains of living things, which float in water and sink to the bottom— for example, mud and sand.

Smelting
Removing an ore from a metal by heating and melting it.

Ultraviolet (UV)
A type of light that is emitted by the Sun. It is invisible to humans but can be seen by some birds and insects.

The Publisher would like to thank the following for permission to reproduce their material. Top = t; Bottom = b; Center = c; Left = l; Right = r
7tl mikeuk/iStock Photo, 7tcl Adiputra/Shutterstock, 7tr, 7cl Evgeny Haritonov/Shutterstock, 7tcr Cylonphoto/iStock Photo, 7cr Aleksey Kurguzov/Shutterstock; 8cr wakila/iStock Photos, 8tc lucentius/iStock Photos, 8cl Susan E. Degginger/Alamy Stock Photo 8cl Yes058 Montree Nanta/Shutterstock, 8tr Norbert Dr. Lange/Alamy Stock Photo; 9tl VvoeVale/iStock Photo, 9cr Norbert Dr. Lange/Alamy Stock Photo, 9cti Steve Bowen/iStock Photo, 9cl CribbVisuals/iStock Photos, 9cli KrimKate/istock Photo, 9clii Roman Tiraspolsky/iStock Photo, 9cr Siim Sepp/Alamy Stock Photo, 9cri Yes058 Montree Nanta/Shutterstock, 9crii Susan E. Degginger/Alamy Stock Photo, 9cr bsiro/Shutterstock; 14t bambambu/Shutterstock, 14tl jxfzsy/iStock Photos, 14c Fokin Oleg/Shutterstock, 14b MediaProduction/iStock Photo; 15tc ivorr/iStock Photos, 15cr Anton Starikov/Shutterstock, 15tr Science History Images/Alamy Stock Photo, 15br vvow/Shutterstock; 16br Kanoke_46/iStock Photos; 21tc mantaphoto/iStock Photo, 21tl thexfilephoto/iStock Photo, 21tr ollo/iStock Photo; 27c akg-images; 28 U.S. Geological Survey. Public domain; 29cl NASA/Carnegie Mellon University/Science Photo Library, 29cr NASA/Science Photo Library; 31t bluecrayola/Shutterstock, 31bl Atmosphere1/Dreamstime, 31cl Mark A Schneider/Dembinsky Photo Associates/Alamy Stock Photo, 31cr PjrStudio/Alamy Stock Photo; 32bcr jrroman/iStock Photos, 32tl Tolga Tezcan/iStock Photos, 32tcl Yauheni Hastsiukhin/Dreamstime,, 32tcr Joyce Photographics/Science Photo Library, 32tr Dong808/iStock Photos, 32bl markrhiggins/iStock Photo, 32bcl Natural History Museum London/Science Photo Library, 32br kavring/Shutterstock; 33tl Dorling Kindersley/Science Photo Library, 33tc Doug McLean/Shutterstock, 33tr gfrandsen/iStock Photo, 33bc Jaroslav Moravcik/Shutterstock, 33br Fossil & Rock Stock Photos/Alamy Stock Photo 33bl Natural History Museum London/Science Photo Library; 34–35 Lukassek/iStock Photo; 38tr Vito Palmisano/iStock Photo, 38tc DCrane08, 38tr Kim Vermaat/iStock Photo, 38br StephanHoerold/iStock Photo; 39tl parameter/iStock Photo, 39b Elen11/iStock Photo; 45cr JacobH/istock Photo.

INDEX

THE AUTHOR & ILLUSTRATOR

EMILY DODD

Emily has always been fascinated by science. She has a degree in geophysical sciences and a master's in communicating science and has written fiction, nonfiction, and TV scripts to share her love of the natural world with children. She loves being outside, drawing, playing soccer, surfing, and wild swimming. She travels widely, taking her interactive science events to schools, libraries, and festivals. Emily lives on the Isle of Skye in Scotland, the perfect place for adventures.

ROBBIE CATHRO

Robbie is an illustrator and storyteller living in Bristol, England, where he creates fun and lively work from his desk in The Island Studios. He loves bright colors and vibrant characters—all of which are inspired from the stories he's given and the animation he loves, as well as the small stories you find in the corner of your day-to-day life. Find more of his work at robbiecathro.com.